Stand UP!

How to Stay True to Yourself

Stand UP!

How to Stay True to Yourself

by Christine Laouénan
illustrated by Cécile Bertrand
edited by Kate O'Dare

sunscreen

Library of Congress Cataloging-in-Publication Data

Laouénan, Christine.
[J'ose pas dire non! English]
Stand up! : how to stay true to yourself / Christine Laouénan ;
illustrated by Cecile Bertrand.
p. cm.
"English translation by Nicholas Elliott."
ISBN 978-1-4197-0198-6
1. Assertiveness in adolescence—Juvenile literature.
I. Bertrand, Cécile, 1953– II. Title.
BF724.3.A77L3613 2012
158.1—dc23
2011039522

Printed and bound in China
10 9 8 7 6 5 4 3 2 1

ABRAMS
THE ART OF BOOKS SINCE 1949
115 West 18th Street
New York, NY 10011
www.abramsbooks.com

contents

ANGER, ATTITUDE, FEAR, CONFIDENCE, LOVE, REJECTION, CONFLICT, DENIAL, CONTROL, BULLYING, EMOTIONS, FEAR, CLOTHES, GOSSIP, TRENDS, PARENTS.

As the title suggests, the purpose of this book is to teach you how to stand up for yourself and learn to say no. We aren't talking about a random "no" shouted at everything you disagree with or don't like. This book is about the opposite kind of "no." The "no" we are talking about is one that you say with a smile and cheerful exclamation point, because this "no" comes from a true, deep part of you. This is a "no" that isn't about rejection, that doesn't come from a fear of making people mad. Instead, it's a "no" that lets you get along with other people while protecting and remaining true to yourself.

The book you're holding does not consist of a list of rules like "If A does this, then B should do that." Rather, it's meant to make you more aware of your own values. Figuring out what these values are, and the good and bad feelings that come along with them, is key to finding your place in the world. The more aware you are, the more you can understand the emotions that get stirred up by conflicts, even little ones, and the better prepared you are to cope.

To get to this point, you've got to do some tinkering. You have to take a look inside, maybe do some rearranging. Think of yourself as a clock: it runs just fine most of the time, but to understand it, to truly know how it works, you need to take it apart and examine all the pieces and see how they go together. Then, when you reassemble the clock, you'll know *exactly* what makes it tick. The process can be a little scary—what if, after taking everything apart, you can't put it back together again? But you can, and doing so will help you get to know yourself better.

the fear of
saying no

No is a plain old one-syllable word, just like yes. But it can be difficult to say. In fact, many people have serious trouble saying no. Even when you know exactly how you feel and have practiced how you are going to say no, the moment comes and you freeze. You stay quiet, or you find yourself saying yes instead. And then you feel bad. You wonder what's wrong with you. Why can't you say what you mean?

Whether you're at home with your family, at school, or with friends, whether you're with adults or people your own age, you can be confronted with a situation that requires you to take a stand. The situations aren't always the same—you might have to accept or refuse, or even negotiate. Of course, there's nothing physically preventing you from expressing your thoughts: you can speak, nod your head, or type them out. But your feelings can be hard to deal with. If you're afraid of what you feel, you won't allow yourself the right to express it. You'll project your fear onto other people: *What right do I have to assert myself like that? What will they think of me if I say no? Will I seem stupid? Uncool? Immature?* If you automatically assume that your "no" will be taken badly, it will be impossible to work up the nerve to say it.

Take Matt, for example. He's a good student, and he doesn't want to share his work with a friend who can't be bothered to do the homework himself. Even worse, this particular friend seems to show up only when he needs something. Matt knows what he wants to say: "No." It doesn't feel that simple, though. Matt thinks, "He's still my friend" and "What if he gets a bad grade? It'll be my fault." The conflict he feels makes it difficult to make a decision.

Matt doesn't want to hurt anyone's feelings, especially a classmate's. He doesn't want to make enemies, and he certainly doesn't want word to get around that he's too scared of getting in trouble to let somebody look at his stupid math homework. Matt's afraid that people will think he's a teacher's

The one thing I can't say no to . . . is chocolate!

pet. So, filled with these conflicting emotions, Matt says yes for the worst possible reason: he's afraid to say no.

Asserting yourself needs to become as natural as breathing. Otherwise, people are always going to get in the way of your personal development. You probably know that, but the fear remains. It's an irrational—but completely understandable—fear of saying what you really think. You know how hard it is because you've felt the conflict inside you, and you probably know how much better you would feel if you did speak your mind. If you knew exactly why you were scared to say no, it would be easier for you to overcome your fears.

Don't feel bad if you've had trouble standing up to someone in the past. Just because you've had trouble before doesn't mean you won't be able to stand up for yourself in the future. You have different relationships with everyone in your life—you might have no problem saying no to one person but absolutely clam up with another. Chances are you feel most comfortable expressing yourself honestly to the people you know best, your immediate circle.

Imagine that your doorbell rings while you're doing your homework. It's a friend asking if you want to hang out. You see this person all the time and know her well. It isn't hard to say no, that you have work to do. It's not personal; you have a commitment—your homework—that you need to fulfill. Yet you might feel totally awkward about asking a different friend to change the time you're supposed to meet because you have to watch your little brother. What's the difference? Why is it easy to be honest in one case but not in another?

There could be many reasons. Maybe the first friend is someone you've known forever and the second friend is new and you want to become closer with him. It's only natural that you won't feel as comfortable with the new friend. The important thing is to learn that it's okay to say no when you feel it's the right thing to do, even if you're nervous about how the person will react. Chances are he'll understand, and if he doesn't, then he probably wouldn't make a very good friend anyway.

saying no to
your parents

It's often easier to say no to people your own age than to those in positions of authority, like your parents. You value your parents' opinions, but sometimes you just don't agree with them. Imagine you've just come back from a class snowboarding trip. You're happy because you went from being an embarrassment on the bunny slope to seriously holding your own on some tricky runs. You want to share this happiness with your parents, but as soon

as you do, your father jumps in. "It takes *years* to get good at skiing, so you'll probably need to keep practicing." Contradicting your father is tricky because it feels as if you're calling into question all his knowledge and experience. But you have convincing arguments: "Dad, it's snowboarding—it's really different from skiing, and you can get good pretty fast." You've asserted your point of view, but suddenly you feel nervous. In challenging your dad, you are not acting like a child; you are declaring, in a small but important way, independence from his ideas. Taking responsibility for your beliefs is a powerful act. It's a lot easier to just stick with a grown-up's opinion and feel safe.

You need the support and affection of your family, and disagreeing with them can make you feel as if you're challenging their love for you. As a result, you're afraid of standing up to them. It may also be true that sometimes you don't get along with your parents. You disagree—internally— with things they say, and maybe you feel guilty about it. This feeling gets turned around inside until you project your own angry feelings onto them. That may be hard to deal with, but it is a huge part of growing up. It's important to learn to separate your parents' thoughts and opinions from your own, and it's important to communicate your feelings to them so they understand where you're coming from.

being yourself

Personalities are built, just like a house. The foundation is laid when you are a kid by what you learn from your parents. Your mom and dad teach you what's right and what's wrong, and what's allowed and what isn't. They teach you the importance of respecting authority. Hopefully, your parents have taught you to be confident in your choices so that you can have authority in your own life. Maybe you've seen plants growing on stakes. Stakes give plants something to lean on as they get stronger. Think of the limits your parents impose on you as a kind of stake. One day you won't need those limits, but for now, they help you grow and define yourself. Part of that process is building up the strength to say no.

When you get older, the heavy construction on your personality begins. You choose from the building materials provided by your parents—some will be essential, and some you'll get rid of. Gradually, you'll start adding your own materials: things you've learned in school or picked up from the books, movies, and music you like. You'll gather knowledge from your experiences with the people and things around you, and you'll put it all together in your own way. A final step in this construction of identity is asserting your own values while still respecting those of your parents.

When you're a teenager, your parents still support you, but you don't always agree with them. One of the most common complaints from teenagers

is that their parents don't listen to them. But teenagers also feel rebellious and angry because they have a hard time expressing themselves to their parents, especially when they're unhappy about something. Thankfully, you can improve this situation by using some simple strategies. First, find the right time to have a conversation; learn to express your views calmly and to really listen to your parents' concerns; and don't be afraid to negotiate. If you interrupt your mom's business call to tell her you don't want to babysit your sister, you aren't going to get what you want. Also, acting sulky or pouty only hurts your cause. It will make your parents doubt your judgment and want to end the conversation quickly. You have the right to express yourself, but if you don't articulate your demands and requests in a sensible way, your chances of being heard go way down!

While it's normal to depend less on your parents as you get older, it's also normal to still require their advice and reassurance. That doesn't make you immature. Meredith, for example, was invited by a friend to go to the house of somebody she didn't know well. She wasn't sure she wanted to go, so she decided to talk to her mom about it. When her mom heard the details—especially that there wouldn't be parents around—she told Meredith she didn't feel comfortable letting her go. Meredith was actually relieved; she didn't feel comfortable going to this person's house either, and she'd been unsure of what to say to her friend.

However, there are times when you will need to assert yourself with your parents. What if your parents want you to be an engineer, but you're

convinced you want to be a sculptor? It might be easier to go along with

what they say, but it's important that you pursue your ambitions. Arya, for

example, has dreamed of being an astronaut his whole life, but his parents

like to drag him back to earth. "Do you know how incredibly difficult it is to

become an astronaut? Try for something more practical." For a while, Arya

agreed with them, but then he realized that if nobody ever pursued his or her

dream, there wouldn't be any astronauts at all! You can realize your dreams if you are willing to work hard to achieve them. It won't be easy, but have you ever noticed how happy you feel when something you've really worked for is successful? You know yourself and you know what will make you happy. Listen to that voice inside you! It's easier to understand and respect other people's desires when you understand your own.

saying no
for yourself

The amount of difficulty you have saying no varies depending on the situation. Anna, for example, takes a stand on all sorts of issues. She speaks out with conviction against racism and sexism, and she offers help when students and teachers are having problems. She knows what she believes in and she's brave about defending her ideals. In fact, she's been president of her class for two years running. But when somebody asks Anna for a pen, even if she needs it herself and it's the only one she has, she hands it over. If her sister asks for another bedtime story, Anna says yes, even though she has a ton of schoolwork. It's strange, because these requests are minor and don't require half the personal commitment of the more significant things that Anna does without a thought.

Anna's issue is that she has adopted a certain persona, or personality, in public that at times conflicts with her own well-being. She thinks of herself as a "righter of wrongs," and as long as she's standing up for others, she has no problem asserting herself. When it comes to defending herself, however, she needs to learn that it is okay to say no.

Jarrod has a different problem. When he's with his family, he lets his older brothers do all the talking and tends to agree with whatever they say. At school, however, Jarrod acts just like his brothers. He's arrogant, and he constantly

interrupts people because he thinks he knows it all. As a result, he's got a reputation for being a bully, and his classmates are starting to avoid him. At home, Jarrod does whatever his brothers tell him. He desperately wants to be like them. He is so concerned about earning their approval that he hasn't figured out what he really believes in.

Sometimes it's hard to say no because the demand being made isn't obvious—it's hidden. For example, Greta has a good friend, Caroline. They're together pretty much all of the time. But for a while now, Greta has been feeling uncomfortable because Caroline acts as if she owns her. Greta can't make new friends without Caroline getting angry and jealous. Caroline also comments on everything Greta does, says, or wears, even when Greta doesn't ask for her opinion. Though Caroline can be a good friend, Greta often feels trapped by the excessive demands Caroline makes on her. Caroline is implicitly saying that if Greta doesn't behave the way that she, Caroline, wants her to, then Greta will lose her as a friend. Something inside Greta keeps her from responding and expressing her feelings, even though she sees what Caroline is doing. She feels powerless and accepts Caroline's behavior.

Since she genuinely likes her friend, Greta feels that she shouldn't deny Caroline anything, because it might hurt her. Greta has resigned herself to their occasionally uncomfortable relationship rather than face her fear of displeasing Caroline and being rejected. She also thinks that friendship means being totally faithful to her friend, no matter what—even to the point of not being able to say no to her.

Greta's done such a good job of meeting Caroline's expectations that she's forgotten how to take her own emotions and needs into account. She has stifled herself so much by putting Caroline first that she has lost a stong sense of her own personality. Sometimes she thinks her passive niceness is part of her personality, but that's not the case at all.

If Greta had known how to stand up to her friend—how to say no to her bossiness without being afraid of disappointing her—she would have remained genuine and been able to remain true to herself as an individual. Although agreement might be nice in the short term, people get tired of someone who always agrees with them and hides his or her true feelings. People need to know you to love you. They can't do that if you're not honest with them.

Sometimes it can be easier to fake your approval or agreement, but in the long term, you pay for not being true to yourself. Your personality changes—and, as a result, so do your relationships with other people. Greta, for example, has already learned to cut off her real feelings in order to not make Caroline angry. Greta has lost confidence in what she feels because she isn't used to listening to herself. She's become a timid girl who profoundly doubts herself. Since she doesn't feel free to make a decision or give her opinion, she is not confident in her choices at all. She is caught in a downward spiral where she cannot say no and doesn't know what she wants. She's become the kind of person who is always ready to help out with friends' emotional problems and listen to secrets, so much so that everyone depends on her, and that gives her a feeling of power over people. She's reassured by this feeling and becomes less and less likely to assert herself and take control of her own life.

Greta needs to go deep inside herself to rediscover what gave her energy and made her happy. If she can do this, she'll be able to use language that allows her to express what she really feels and reconnect with her true identity. If she doesn't succeed, she'll become more frustrated. By pushing aside her real feelings, she's created a deep pool of resentment—a pool that might turn into an angry geyser if she doesn't figure out how to express herself! Rather than being angry with herself, Greta may be angry with the people around her. This makes sense to her, since she doesn't have a clear sense of how the problem started in the first place. It's much easier to take out your frustration and anger on the people around you than face the true problem. It's important to remember that feelings of fear and powerlessness are often at the root of what causes us to be angry and withdraw, and in the end we only hurt ourselves and the people we care about by giving into those feelings.

respecting yourself

Sometimes it can be hard to assert yourself when it comes to personal and physical experiences like love and sex. It can be confusing and embarrassing to talk about them. But it's important to do what is best for you and to talk about what's bothering you.

For example, Julia is a ninth grader whose boyfriend is in another grade at the same school. They used to be more affectionate at school, but Julia got uncomfortable because her classmates were always teasing her. Julia felt conflicted. If she really liked this guy, why did it bother her that people made jokes about them being together? Julia was confused enough that she went to the school's guidance counselor, who reassured her that if she wanted to keep her relationship more private, that was her business, and that being bothered by people's comments was normal because it could be difficult to ignore one's peers and friends.

It's equally important to recognize if you are feeling pressured by your friends or your boyfriend or girlfriend about sex. They need to know that you have limits and that you won't do anything—or listen to any teasing—that makes you uncomfortable.

There may also be times when this inappropriate behavior extends beyond teasing. For example, some boys were bullying Elise at her middle school. They'd do stuff like throw her bag on the ground and stand around to watch as she picked it up. They'd also make rude comments about her body, and sometimes they'd act as if they were going to grab her or touch her.

Elise had the courage to stand up for herself and respect her own feelings, and she told a teacher. By doing this, she didn't just protect herself; she helped the whole school. Her tormentors were punished, which meant that they were forced to confront the impact of their inappropriate behavior.

Mark also had a bad experience. One day he was sitting on a park bench, reading a book and not paying much attention, when a man sat down next to him. A few minutes later, the man leaned over and touched Mark's arm in a way that made him feel uncomfortable. Mark didn't hesitate: he grabbed his bag and ran. When he got home, he told his parents about what had happened.

No matter how aware you are of your surroundings, you may one day

encounter someone who behaves inappropriately toward you. The person might be a stranger, or someone you know. No matter who this person is, no matter where you are, you must speak out to prevent yourself from being abused. Run, scream, call for help, and *do not be embarrassed*. The fault lies with the other person; you are completely in the right.

Sometimes even the strongest reaction isn't enough to stop someone who's intent on committing sexual violence. If you're a victim of assault, don't keep it to yourself! Talk to someone you trust—a relative, an adult at school, a classmate—and tell him or her what happened without feeling ashamed or guilty. Often, abusers will try and convince their victims that

they were somehow to blame for the abuse. Never believe it. Remember that no matter what happened or who did it, you were abused. Don't feel guilty and don't be swayed by instances in which the person is nice to you; some people are experts at using psychological manipulation to get what they want. They may compliment you or even give you gifts. They may seem so friendly and harmless that you don't want to refuse them. But they have no right to make you feel uncomfortable, no matter how nice they seem sometimes, and you have every right to stand up for yourself.

Although it is okay to keep some things to yourself, some secrets are too heavy not to share. They create darkness and pain inside you. These secrets need to be shared with an adult, even if the idea of talking about them seems horrible. Bringing out the truth will take a great weight off you.

Any kind of assault can have lasting consequences. The real problems arise, though, when you don't get help and support. It's shocking, but the fact is that many women and men have gone through the same thing. Talking about it with a person you trust will allow you to move on from the experience.

You should also talk about the abuse because the law is on your side and your abuser can be sent to prison for what he or she did. An abuser uses his or her power over you and disrespects your body. Your body is your property and yours alone—absolutely no one has the right to touch it without your permission. You should feel proud of your body, and also responsible for it. You need to have enough self-confidence to protect yourself from dangerous situations, even if they involve kids your age.

If a friend tells you that he or she has been abused, listen with an open mind. Make your friend feel safe and confident that he or she can trust you with this information. Remind your friend that a victim of abuse shouldn't feel guilty. You could say, "I know how upsetting this is, but it isn't your fault. This person did something wrong, something that's against the law. Lots of people have gone through this, and we can get you help." The best thing you can do is support your friend. What you shouldn't do is try to solve the crime, so to speak, on your own. This is a legal matter, and should be handled by trustworthy adults.

When it comes to protecting yourself, it's helpful to develop a few strategies for dealing with potentially risky situations. When you're going out, tell your parents where you're going, whom you're going to meet, how you're getting there, and when you'll be back. Your parents should always know where you are. If you're going to a party or a concert, travel with friends rather than go alone. Stay away from dark places, like parks, at night. Abusers know how to identify vulnerable people and situations. It's a whole lot easier to attack someone who's alone at night in a park than someone in the middle of a crowded mall. If a stranger drives up and asks for directions, move away from the vehicle before answering, or if you feel uncomfortable, don't answer at all. Do not feel bad about refusing requests for help if you feel uncomfortable or suspicious in any way.

why saying
no is hard

Have you ever heard people talk about a conflict between their heart and their head? That their heart—or emotions—wants one thing, but their head—or rational mind—knows that it isn't possible? These types of conflicts can make it very difficult to express what you want because you truly want two different things! In cases like this, it's important to cut yourself some emotional slack. To figure out what's best for you, you need to listen to yourself and make sure that other people are listening to you, too. It will take some practice. You'll take one step at a time until nothing can stand in your way.

Imagine that you are all alone flying your personal plane. There are tons of blinking instruments in front of you; they represent your emotions, both pleasant and unpleasant. When one of your desires isn't met, a red light goes on. As a pilot, you must recognize this signal and take appropriate action. At home, maybe your parents are always holding up your sister as a role model. You love your sister, but sometimes you wish your parents would

recognize that you are your own person. You need to express your feelings to your parents! The red light is going on, and you need to tell them that what they are doing is not only unhelpful; it's also hurting you.

What if you decide simply to give hints about how you feel, without spelling it out? Sorry, that's no good. If you only tell half the truth, people will only half understand you! Whatever you do, avoid negative thoughts like, "Why should I bother telling anyone? They won't understand anyway." That type of thinking will prolong your suffering. Trust your family and friends to listen to you. You can't expect them to guess what's wrong. Once you talk to them, they will be able to do a better job of helping you to appreciate your best qualities and understand your strengths.

Think of all those times you've said no without any trouble. Store those memories in your mind for when you need a reminder that you can do it. You should also think about the situations where it isn't so easy to say no. You can't stand up to your big brother, who's always been quick to tell you you're wrong and put you down? Ask yourself why you're afraid of him. Is it his authority? A fear of rejection? Asking these questions is the first step to asserting yourself better. You need to know exactly what you're up against before you can defend yourself.

Imagine yourself as a mythic hero about to set out on a journey. The world you are entering is filled with traps and danger. These are the obstacles you need to overcome to discover yourself. You can move through this world at your own pace; there's no need to rush. Each time you stand up for yourself, freely and comfortably, you'll notice that you've gained some inner strength and that you haven't alienated your friends and family.

Practice by saying no in low-pressure situations. This will make it easier when tougher situations arise. Don't get discouraged if at first it doesn't go well, or if, despite your best intentions, you can't quite say no yet. Keep trying. Your dad wants you to go jogging with him, but you'd rather

see your friends? That's a tough one. Maybe this Sunday you go running, but you negotiate a visit to the movies with your friends for next Sunday. Compromise can be a good way to solve problems.

When you start asserting yourself, you may also have the opposite experience. Perhaps the first time you say no, it goes fine, but the second time you try, it doesn't. If that's the case, don't feel guilty—it is hard to accomplish things when you feel bad. Remember that old piece of wisdom: If at first you don't succeed, try, try again!

To be able to say no with confidence, you also need to understand what you're saying no to. Obvious, right? But it isn't always so clear. Sometimes may feel you feel confused about a situation and not sure what the other person's intentions are.

For example, you and your friend Max are supposed to go mountain biking. The night before, Max announces that he's invited someone you don't get along with. Give yourself some time to think before you respond. A hasty response could end up starting a fight with Max and making you feel worse.

Ask yourself why Max didn't consult you before inviting this other person. Why did he tell you only when it was a done deal?

If you take some time to reflect, you won't feel backed into a corner, and you'll be able to articulate exactly what's bothering you. You'll be able to stand up to Max: "Listen, when we planned this trip, it was going to be just you and me. But now you've invited Chris, and you know we don't get along, so I don't feel comfortable going."

If you don't tell Max this kind of behavior is unacceptable to you, he'll keep being inconsiderate—he'll get used to you saying yes to whatever he decides. Don't get forced into always playing the "nice" one and not saying what you think!

Sometimes you don't want to say no because you're worried about what the other person's reaction will be. The less comfortable you feel saying no, the more worried you'll feel. In a way, you become afraid of feeling afraid. Yet most of the time, you'll realize that the other person can't really do anything to hurt you. Your fears actually have very little basis in reality. Have you heard President Franklin Delano Roosevelt's famous declaration, "The only thing we have to fear is fear itself"? Realizing that you are afraid of feeling afraid usually makes you *less* afraid. And that's liberating!

Saying no does not mean acting like a spoiled brat. It doesn't mean stamping your feet and shouting demands—if you go that route, you'll be in for some seriously stormy conflicts! That kind of aggressive approach usually ends with both sides angry and convinced that they're in the right.

Instead, take some time to think over your position. Be completely sure of what you want so you can feel confident saying no but not get wrapped up in emotion, which often leads to treating the other person disrespectfully. People who really know what they believe have no trouble finding arguments to support their positions.

During winter vacation, your parents always send you to visit your aunt who lives at the beach. Several times you've asked if you could go snowboarding instead, but they never go for it, and you end up at your aunt's again. This time, though, you're determined: "I know a snowboarding trip

is expensive. I'll do odd jobs around the house to help out financially." Your parents will be happy that you're showing initiative and will be impressed that you understand their position and their needs. Your taking a stand leads to an engaging discussion for all of you.

Since you were able to stand up for what you wanted, you were also able to address your parents' concerns—snowboarding is expensive—and respond to them constructively. Maybe next year you'll happily take the bus to see your aunt. Once it becomes easy for you to stand up for yourself, you'll be able to hear other people's "no" without feeling attacked. Just because someone doesn't agree with you doesn't mean they're rejecting you. Your friends and your family still care for you, even when they turn you down.

When you have reached the point where someone else's "no" won't undermine your self-confidence, you'll be able to actually listen to other people's concerns, and process exactly what kinds of things other people say yes or no to. This understanding will allow you to be more honest. If you feel confident and at peace with your decisions, you'll be able to build richer and more genuine relationships with other people.

express yourself!

During middle school and high school, you really begin to build your future identity. You start to differentiate yourself from your parents and move toward becoming your own person. If you don't feel confident about standing up for yourself, you'll miss out on a lot of important experiences that this time in your life offers. Some of these experiences will be complicated, even difficult to deal with, but you need to handle them on your way to becoming an adult.

Take Georgia, for example, for a few months now, she has been getting bad grades. One night after asking about school, her mother burst into tears and said, "I can't sleep at all because of you." Since then, Georgia has felt really guilty. She hates the idea that her mom is up all night worrying about

What are you doing?

Growing.

her. She wants to protect her mom and not make her miserable. This concern makes Georgia feel pressured, even trapped. Even though Georgia wishes she could discuss her problems with her mom, she doesn't, for fear of adding to her mom's anxiety. So she goes off to school without saying anything, and every day feels tougher and tougher.

The fact that Georgia has problems is normal at her age. Who wouldn't, when so much is going on physically, intellectually, and emotionally? But by allowing her mother to blame her for the fact that she can't sleep at night, Georgia is doing herself a disservice. Her own emotional needs take a backseat to her mom's.

Georgia needs to speak frankly to her mother and tell her how she feels: "Mom, I know it's important to you that I do well in school—it's important to me, too—but I don't like the way you tell me you're worried. You make it sound like it's my job to study hard just to keep you from feeling bad." Of course, a big part of your parents' job is watching over your education; they should help you when you're having trouble and discipline you if you aren't working hard enough. But if you are truly doing your best, then that's all they can ask of you.

Alex is also dealing with a complicated situation. His parents are divorced. He's at his dad's house two weekends a month, and when he's there, his father is constantly bad-mouthing his mom. When he goes back to his mom's, she interrogates him: "Is your dad dating?" and "What did he say?" and "What did you two do together?"

Alex feels caught in the cross fire. His parents are angry at each other, and they're using him to express their unhappiness. He's already sad that they've divorced, and now he has to deal with their anger at each other all the time. It makes him feel extremely lonely.

Alex has the right to stand up to his parents: "Don't do this to me. I love both of you, and you're both trying to force me into a role I won't play. And it makes me feel terrible to hear you say nasty things about each other! I need to know that you think about my feelings and that I can count on you. You're separated, but you're both still my parents."

Georgia and Alex are in tough positions. They both need to identify exactly what's bothering them and then express it to their parents, the major authority figures in their lives. Right now, they feel like prisoners; they can't be honest and are suffering because of it. They're under real emotional pressure. In order to mature, they must stand up for themselves. Only then can they have an honest relationship with their parents. If talking to their parents is too daunting, they need to seek out another trusted adult, like a relative or a teacher.

don't let others
control you!

"Why's your dress so tight? You look silly." James is getting ready to go to the movies with his girlfriend, Stephanie, and he's adamant. "I won't go out with you when you're wearing that outfit!" Finally, Stephanie puts on jeans and a sweatshirt. By giving in, she sends the message to James that he can control her. But what James is doing is wrong. His own insecurity makes him try to pull Stephanie down, and he's being a bully. He comes up with a

bunch of excuses for his behavior: "She's my girlfriend, so I can judge what does and doesn't look good on her." Basically, James convinces himself that he's actually doing something good for her.

But what about Stephanie? Maybe James is feeding off her fear that she isn't as pretty as she'd like to be. Now, under constant pressure from James, she's having trouble deciding what really is best for her. James undermines her and prevents her from freely expressing who she is. If she lets him keep up this criticism, it could threaten her self-confidence. James's behavior is unacceptable, and Stephanie must put a stop to it.

Of course, James doesn't just interfere in how Stephanie dresses. He's also critical of her friends. Molly? "She's a annoying." And Richard, her lab partner? "Lame, and fat, too." Gradually, James is alienating Stephanie from her friends and gaining control over whom she socializes with. He's not only

possessive, he's also jealous, a feeling that he thinks is proof of love—which it absolutely is not. Jealousy makes him try to control Stephanie and use emotional blackmail to get his way: "If you loved me, you wouldn't do that." James's jealousy shows that he is disturbed by the fact that Stephanie has her own life. But Stephanie lets James dominate her because she's afraid he'll break up with her if she doesn't. The longer she lets this go on, the less she'll feel able to stop him. Sometimes James knows he's gone too far and he'll apologize—maybe he'll even give Stephanie a present. But this is just another way of manipulating her feelings.

Attempting to control someone goes against a fundamental human

right: respect. To respect someone means that you recognize him or her as a human being with feelings and concerns. When people feel respected, they feel confident in their own identity, and it is easier for them to return this respect. It's a building block of social engagement: I respect you because you respect me; you respect me because I respect you. Each person in this exchange understands the importance of the other. The respect you show to someone else comes back to you.

Finally, Stephanie gets sick of James's attempts to control her, and she breaks up with him. For revenge, he starts spreading rumors about her. He's trying to destroy her reputation because she rejected him and he can't stand not having control over her. By bad-mouthing Stephanie, James is abusing the trust she put in him when they were together and also undermining her faith in her future partners.

James doesn't stop at spreading rumors. Whenever he sees Stephanie, he insults her and calls her names. Stephanie feels ashamed and humiliated. She isn't sure what to do and thinks about shouting insults back at him. She doesn't, though, because she doesn't want to play his game. Finally, one morning she takes him aside and addresses the issue head-on: "I will not accept you insulting me like this. What you're saying really hurts. We aren't together anymore, but why can't you respect what we once had?" Stephanie has every right to speak to him this way. It is important for her to assert herself and say no to such poor treatment.

say no to bullying!

Dan is a good student, but he lacks self-confidence. Lately he's become the target of two boys in his class, John and Anthony, who constantly bully and harass him. Dan hasn't said a word to anyone about the bullying. But he bursts into tears in front of the whole class one day when John and Anthony do something particularly cruel. As if he didn't already feel bad enough, breaking down in front of everybody makes Dan retreat even further into his shell. He constantly berates himself and asks, "Why am I so weak? Why can't I stop them? What's wrong with me?" But he's unable to fight back.

John and Anthony take advantage of Dan's weakened state. The fact that their classmates have seen the power they have over Dan makes them feel stronger, and they behave even worse. They continue their "Torture Dan" campaign. A stumble in gym class, a new sweater, even a too-clean backpack turns into material for these bullies, and poor Dan still can't fight back. Now his grades are suffering. Have John and Anthony won?

Dan gradually becomes a nobody in the eyes of his classmates. Some of them even think that he deserves the bad treatment. None of them want to be in his position, so they go along with tormenting him. Teenagers will often follow stronger classmates rather than risk becoming targets themselves. Although individually they may disagree with what's happening, they stay quiet and allow the victim to keep suffering. In a completely unequal struggle—Dan versus his classmates—his tormentors feel tough, even though what they're doing is really cowardly.

How can Dan escape from this terrible situation, which is causing him so much pain? How can he stand up to all his classmates when he has no support at all? There is a way. Dan has to get over the fear of his tormentors and remove himself from the cycle of bullying. Easier said than done, right?

It isn't easy, but the key is for Dan to truly accept himself. If Dan takes himself seriously, so will other people. He needs to ask why he lets John and Anthony dominate him. Dan doesn't like himself; he feels weak and has gone along with the bullying because deep down—and totally incorrectly—he worries they might be right about him.

Dan needs to get some self-confidence back to believe it when he says to himself, "This isn't my fault. The problem here is with the people attacking me. They aren't good students, and they resent that I am. It's easy for them to take out their frustrations on me. But that's going to change, because I'm not their doormat."

If Dan can't get his self-confidence back, then there's a real chance that he'll begin to identify with his tormentors. That means he'll start feeling as if he's responsible for what they're doing to him. And then he'll feel guilty for being a victim—that he's the one causing the abuse. To keep that from happening, Dan needs to stop saying to himself, "They attack me because I'm a loser." This negative thinking makes him complicit in his own victimization.

Once Dan realizes what he needs to do, he should find some classmates who are like him and aren't interested in the bullying that John and Anthony

enjoy. When Dan approaches people individually, he may find that they are more reasonable and sympathetic. If that doesn't work, Dan must turn to a trusted adult at school or speak to his parents. They're there to help!

He also needs to call on the classmates who meekly follow along when John and Anthony tell them what to do. They need to be aware that this kind of behavior can have terrible consequences. Throughout history, many people have gone along with strong leaders only to realize later that they turned a blind eye to terrible violence and cruelty. If they're acting as part of a group, they feel that their personal responsibility disappears. But it doesn't.

Since they feel vulnerable, people lacking confidence often want to join groups. In a way, it lets them hide, blend in, and even feel safe. It's okay to some extent to feel comforted by the reassurance of your peers, but you

must remember to never let go of your own judgment just to get along with a group. Your instincts and experiences shape who you are, and you need to trust your feelings.

Remember that people who enjoy attacking others aren't tough. Ask yourself why bullies act the way they do. What are they trying to show? What kind of weakness is this behavior designed to hide? Most often you'll see that, for whatever reason, the bullies themselves feel vulnerable. But you know what? That's no excuse.

Dan is harassed by bullies who are using him as a way to express their own frustrations. This kind of violence is irrational, like other forms of discrimination, such as racism and sexism. Do you think it's okay for somebody to be excluded because they're a different color, gender, or religion?

Discriminatory behavior violates an individual's fundamental rights. If you're a victim of discrimination at school, learn how to defend your rights and calmly stand up for yourself. Don't ever let the person bothering you think that he or she can get away with it. By reacting calmly, you'll also deny bullies the pleasure of watching you get angry. Responding to aggression with aggression almost never works. Instead, try to talk to the offender—if you can—and then take the matter up with a teacher or adult. If you feel unsafe talking to the aggressor, ask someone you trust for help! Protecting yourself is most important.

say no to trends!

Going through puberty can be an awkward time. There's so much happening with your body that you can feel vulnerable. It makes sense that you want to get closer to people your own age, people who are going through the same things. You may want to dress a certain way to show that you're part of a certain crowd. You might even adopt the same way of walking and talking as your friends, or visit the same websites and read the same blogs, or play the same video games. Doing all these things feels good, as though you've left childhood behind and now have new, teenage tastes. But are you making these choices freely?

I like this shirt, but it's out of style.　　I'd really like to get a striped shirt . . .　　But polka dots ar[e] so in right now.

At school, people wear designer clothes in part because they like how they look but also to broadcast to other teens that they know the latest trends. Fashion is all about trends that change quickly, and if you don't keep up, you'll look out of style. When stores put out their new merchandise for spring, you might be annoyed to see that the dress or shirt you bought last year and loved now looks totally dated. So you come up with the best arguments you can think of to convince your mom or dad to let you buy new stuff—spending money is now essential. You're afraid of not being on the trendy, so you go to the opposite extreme and buy all the latest fashions you can afford. You want to be the first to have something and also the first to stop wearing it when the trend catches on with other people and doesn't seem so cool anymore.

And I want to be trendy!

Fashionable!

So polka dots it is.

Advertisers want you to feel the pressure to be fashionable because it means you'll spend money. They know exactly what to say to convince you that you need to buy X, Y, or Z to be beautiful or handsome. Buy this pair of pants and you'll be magically transformed! At your age, when so much is changing and you feel so unsettled, you may be especially vulnerable to these types of claims.

Suddenly, you believe that some new product is exactly what you need to be cool. In order to sell things, advertisers don't pull any punches; they want you to feel insecure if you don't buy their products. They want you to look at photoshopped models and feel bad so that you'll buy more shampoo or deodorant or whatever they're selling. They want you to feel that the answer to all your problems is buying their product.

The whole point of advertising is to get into your head so you don't question what you're being told—you just want the product without really thinking about it. The ultimate trick of advertising is getting you to confuse the importance of *being* with the importance of *having.* What matters is how you live, your being, and not the stuff you accumulate. Stay sharp and analyze the methods that advertisements are using to make you feel a certain way. If you wear fashionable clothes to feel good about yourself, you're going to be dependent on other people looking at you and noticing you. But what if they don't? Then what? The more you dress for other people, or do anything that requires recognition to be meaningful, the less you'll be able to make choices that are just about what you want.

So learn to stand up to any attempt to make you look or dress a certain way. You have to trust yourself enough to know what suits you and what you really want. Take a look around you—you'll see that the people who are most eager to conform are the people with the least confidence. The more secure people feel, the less likely they are to get stuck following trends.

It's all about balance. You can find a look that's your own even at the local mall where everybody

else shops. Think about what you like best about yourself, and dress in a way that highlights those features. Don't beat yourself up if your body doesn't fit some imaginary standard. You're unique—be proud of it!

To be happy with yourself when you're a teenager, or later as an adult, you have to make choices based on what you want, not what you are told to want. Discovering what you like, your good points and your bad, is a big part of maturing. Remember, clothing isn't you. You aren't what you wear!

There will be days when you look in the mirror and say, "Ugh." But you know what? You need to stand up for yourself . . . even *to* yourself! Practice focusing on what you like, not the million little "flaws" that nobody else notices. So don't be afraid: set out to discover yourself. Celebrate your strengths, express what makes you different, and play the cards you were dealt. To be a fulfilled adult, you need to be calling the shots about how you want to live. A big part of that is feeling strong and secure. And a big part of feeling strong and secure is standing up for you.

it's okay to
be angry

You have the right to get angry, and you don't have to say no to expressing that anger. Anger isn't necessarily good or bad; sometimes it just is. And when you're trying to find ways to stand up for yourself against the people and things that make you feel bad, the process can be very frustrating. So sometimes we need to get angry as a way of getting feelings out; otherwise they might stay inside us and ultimately cause more harm. Buried,

or repressed, anger is like a time bomb—at some point it will go off, and you'll have no control over when it does. Or think of it as a pressure cooker: that pressure needs to escape!

Just as it can be hard to stand up for yourself, it can also be hard to get angry. You might feel that if you get angry with someone, you'll lose the person's love or friendship. That fear is normal, but you still need to be able to express your anger when necessary, but in a constructive way. As long as you don't go overboard, the person will be able to understand how he or she has upset you.

But how can you express anger without directly attacking other people?

One way is by being honest about the pain you're in and making them face their responsibility for causing it: "You did this to me, and it really hurt. You had no right to do that. How would you feel if I did the same thing to you?" You are criticizing their actions, not them as people.

Don't be afraid of anger. Conflict is part of interacting with other people, and it's a huge part of life. Everyone has a right to get angry and express his or her feelings. In some cases, it may be the only way to exchange opinions with someone. Asserting yourself and letting others know how you feel can be a good thing as long as you do so in a way that is clear and doesn't demean other people.

confidence is
key

Now that you know the whys, hows, and whens of saying no, remember them the next time you're in a tough situation. Have confidence in who you are and what you believe in, and you'll find that saying no can be empowering!

suggestions for further reading

Books

Cooper, Scott. *Speak Up and Get Along!: Learn the Mighty Might, Thought Crop, and More Tools to Make Friends, Stop Teasing, and Feel Good About Yourself.* Free Spirit Publishing, 2005.

Humphrey, Sandra McLeod and Brian Strassburg. *Hot Issues, Cool Choices: Facing Bullies, Peer Pressure, Popularity, and Put-downs.* Prometheus Books, 2007.

Kaufman, Gershen and Lev Raphael and Pamela Espeland. *Stick Up for Yourself: Every Kid's Guide to Personal Power & Positive Self-Esteem.* Free Spirit Publishing, 1999.

Moss, Wendy L. *Being Me: A Kid's Guide to Boosting Confidence and Self-esteem.* Magination Press, 2010.

Palmer, Pat and Melissa Alberti Froehner. *Teen Esteem: A Self-Direction Manual for Young Adult.* Impact Publishers, 2010.

Websites

http://askthejudge.info

www.dosomething.com

www.kidshealth.org

www.pacerkidsagainstbullying.org

www.stopbullying.gov

index

difficulties, difficulty:
    expressing yourself and, 45
    in saying no, 35–43
    and saying no for yourself,
      24–25
discovering yourself:
    and saying no to trends, 67
    why saying no is hard and, 37
discriminatory behavior, 24, 60
divorce, 47–48
doubt, 27

E

embarrassment, 29, 31
emotions:
    and anger as okay, 69, 71
    being yourself and, 23
    and control by others, 53, 55
    expressing yourself and, 17,
      27, 46–49
    and fear of saying no, 10–14
    respecting yourself and, 30–31
    and saying no for yourself,
      25–27
    and saying no to bullying, 60
    values and, 9
    why saying no is hard and,
      35–41
expressing yourself:
    anger and, 21, 27, 48, 71
    fear and, 13, 21, 46
    parents and, 17, 21, 44–49
    respecting yourself and, 29,
      31–33
    and saying no for yourself, 27
    why saying no is hard and,
      36–37

F

family:
    being yourself and, 21
    expressing yourself and, 49

    and fear of saying no, 10, 13
    and saying no for yourself, 24–25
    and saying no to parents, 17
    why saying no is hard and,
      36–37, 41–43
fears, fear:
    and anger as okay, 70–71
    being yourself and, 21
    and control by others, 52–53
    expressing yourself and, 13,
      21, 46
    of saying no, 10–14
    and saying no for yourself, 26–27
    and saying no to bullying, 57
    and saying no to parents, 17
    and saying no to trends, 62, 67
    why saying no is hard and, 37, 40
friends, friendship:
    and anger as okay, 70
    being yourself and, 21
    and control by others, 50–55
    and fear of saying no, 10–14
    respecting yourself and, 31–32
    and saying no for yourself, 25–27
    and saying no to parents, 16
    and saying no to trends, 61
    why saying no is hard and,
      37–40, 43
frustration:
    and anger as okay, 68
    and saying no for yourself, 27
    and saying no to bullying, 58, 60

G

guilt:
    expressing yourself and, 45
    respecting yourself and, 31–32,
      34
    and saying no to bullying, 58
    and saying no to parents, 17
    why saying no is hard and, 38